Mis-takes

I Tried and I'm Proud of It!

Jenna Bayne

Balboa Press books may be ordered through booksellers or by contacting:

Balboa Press
A Division of Hay House
1663 Liberty Drive
Bloomington, IN 47403
www.balboapress.com
1 (877) 407-4847

ISBN: 978-1-5043-8628-9 (sc)
ISBN: 978-1-5043-8629-6 (e)

Library of Congress Control Number: 2017912784

Print information available on the last page.

Balboa Press rev. date: 08/22/2017

BALBOA
PRESS
A DIVISION OF HAY HOUSE

Dedication

This book is dedicated to Dr. Wayne Dyer. You have taught me that everything in life is an interpretation, and how I choose to interpret life is up to me. Thank you for your wisdom.

"Change the way you see things, and the things you see change." Dr. Wayne Dyer

A Message from The Author

Dear Friend,

I am so happy that our life paths have crossed. I hope that the message of this book brings you laughter and ease as you remember to celebrate your *Mis-takes*. My intention is to bring you back to life's basic truths. To remind you that the *Mis-takes* you make are nothing more than results produced from your experiences. How you choose to use your results will either propel you forward or keep you stuck. It is not the mis-takes that you make but what you do with them that matters. You have the power.

You are not here to get everything right. You are here to live, learn and grow. We do not know what lies ahead or what the best course of action always is to take. And, this is the beauty of life. Life is risky and uncertain, and also full of beauty and amazement if we allow ourselves to see it.

I encourage you to allow yourself and those in your life to make *Mis-takes*. *Mis-takes* mean progress, and progress means that you are learning to become better than who you've ever been before. Everything is okay. You are okay. Life is magnificent. And, you are exactly where you need to be in this very moment. Don't give up, don't back down. Keep your head up, know what you know and keep moving forward.

I can't wait to celebrate life with YOU!

"A life spent making mistakes is not only more honorable, but more useful than a life spent doing nothing." - George Bernard Shaw

With deepest admiration,
Jenna

A Message to all Influencers of Children

First, I would like to appreciate you for doing the best that you can in every moment. Being a human is interesting. We stress over things that don't need to be stressed over, we care about things that don't really matter and we often care way too much what others think about us.

If you take time to sit back and think about all the things you have stressed over, all the moments you worried for no reason, and all the times you were angry – you will realize just how ridiculous us humans can be. Think of the value that came out of the mis-takes that you've made and how these challenges have influenced who you have become. You are not perfect nor should you try to be. All you need to be is you. You, are the perfect you, our world needs! So, thank you for being here.

My wish for all of you, influencers of children, is for you to have a little more fun. There will be moments as an influencer where you will question your ability to do a good job. It is natural for you to have moments where you feel inadequate, helpless, and frustrated, and you will lose your patience at times. You will curse your job, dislike your body and argue with your partner every now and then. And, this is all okay. This is actually part of being human. Be easy on yourself. Love yourself a little more. This contrasting life experienced is actually a gift. It allows you to gain clarity and understanding about what you really do want.

As an influencer of children, you have to **be** the person you want your children to grow to be. It is your job to equip our youth with the necessary tools and strategies that will help them become the people they are meant to become. The BayneBooks® Series is here to help you do this.

The BayneBook® Series is a children's book series created to teach valuable life strategies and leaderships skills to our future generations. Each book represents one concept constructed in a way to support the neurological development of young minds to establish a healthy foundation for positive self-esteem and confidence. In other words, the BayneBooks® Series are tangible, leadership-strategy tools disguised as entertaining children's books. They are meant to bond you with the children in your life, while actively engaging in personal growth. To help support you with going deeper with the book message, there are magical companion tools such as games, worksheets and exercises. For access to these materials check out jennabayne.com

Mis-takes is the third book in the BayneBooks® Series. It is about redefining what a mistake is and what it means for you and your children. In other words, mistakes are really "miss takes". They are experiences we all have that produced a result. Every result produced provides us with an opportunity to learn, and a chance to try again with a little more knowledge in our pockets than we have ever had before. It is not the mis-take, but what we do with it that matters. Remember that the most beautiful stones found in nature are those that have been weathered. In the same way, every experience that you have molds the beautiful soul that you are. *Mis-takes* are beautiful gifts. Relax. Breathe. Celebrate!

This book is a gift for YOU because you are great!

Dear_____,

Mis-takes are great
please know this is true.
Celebrate with me,
and I will celebrate with you!

We are celebrating life
and all of its glory!
By trying new things
we create our life story.

This is about us
being a team,
living this life
to the fullest extreme!

I cherish you friend,
I couldn't do this alone.
You are my bestie, my rock,
my backbone!

One thing I love about you is:

_____

Thanks for being you!

Yours truly,

Mis-takes

I Tried and I'm Proud of It!

Mistake is just one word
I like to split in two.
Mistake becomes mis-take
not meaning to confuse.

When mis-take is read as two words
it is pronounced, "miss take".
Mis-takes are how I learn
no matter what mis-takes I make.

Mistakes are often seen as negative
like I did something wrong,
but, *mis-takes* are part learning
and learning is lifelong.

Mis-takes are opportunities
to learn all that I can,
when I make a mis-take
I get to revise a brand new plan.

Woohoo, I made a mis-take!
I have learned because I tried.
I took a chance, and I will try again,
I am who I am with pride!

When I am learning
I sometimes feel sad,
like when the mark on my paper
shows a mark that is bad.

I sometimes feel embarrassed,
I feel I am not good enough.
I sometimes get angry
when life seems really tough.

Sometimes I miss the pass
or fail to get a goal.
Sometimes I make a mistake
and I want sink into a hole.

And, then I remember
that it was just a mis-take!
It would be worse if I did not try.
It is time I celebrate!

Woohoo, I made a mis-take!
I have learned because I tried.
I took a chance, and I will try again,
I am who I am with pride!

Failure is a great thing!
"Bad" marks do not exist.
Challenges are just signs for me
to learn and then persist.

I cannot be a failure
because I will always learn and grow
I will take action and continue
to build on what I know.

Challenges make me who I am
and I becoming someone great.
I have so much to offer this world
I will show you just you wait!

Everybody makes mis-takes,
adults make them too,
these are life experiences
we all have to go through!

Woohoo, I made a mis-take!
I have learned because I tried.
I took a chance, and I will try again,
I am who I am with pride!

Mis-takes
I Tried and I'm Proud of It!

Extra, Extra!
There is so much
more to discover!

Grab your cuddle buddy and head to jennabayne.com to download complementary and fun companion materials to learn more about celebrating Mis-takes.

You will:

- Discover the beauty in your Mis-takes
- How to remain positive even when it feels hard
- Explore a guided meditation to keep you mentally strong
- Learn ways to teach others how to celebrate their mis-takes
- Hear directly from the author

JOIN THE

52/5
CHALLENGE

52 WEEKS
OF 5 MINUTE
CHALLENGES

THAT WILL EQUIP YOU
WITH THE STRATEGIES AND TECHNIQUES

TO ♥VE THE PEOPLE
IN YOUR LIFE BETTER.

BEGIN THE CHALLENGE AT
JENNABAYNE.COM/525

About the Author

Jenna Bayne is the size of a mouse but has the heart of a lion. She began as a classroom teacher in Ontario, Canada, while building her own virtual coaching practice dealing with disordered eating habits among teens and adults. Through her exposure working with young adults, she quickly identified a series of self-limiting challenges that continued to be brought to their one on one coaching sessions. From this insight and her deep understanding of how to support the educational system, she recognized the need for tangible resources to address and help to overcome these self-limiting beliefs at younger ages. Thus, BayneBooks® Series was born. Find out more about her nutritional courses, BayneBooks® companion materials and all other things Jenna at jennabayne.com.

CPSIA information can be obtained
at www.ICGtesting.com
Printed in the USA
BVHW02s1714070718
521006BV00011B/72/P

9 781504 386289